HOCKEY
How It Works

The Science of Sports The Science of Sports

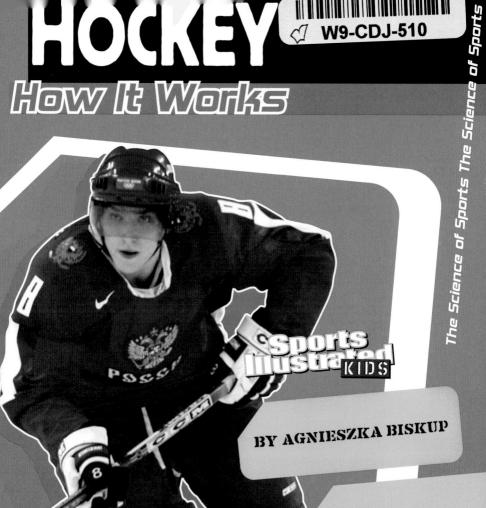

Sports Illustrated KIDS

BY AGNIESZKA BISKUP

Consultant:
Alain Haché
Department of Physics
University of Moncton,
New Brunswick, Canada

CAPSTONE PRESS
a capstone imprint

Sports Illustrated KIDS The Science of Sports is published by Capstone Press,
1710 Roe Crest Drive, North Mankato, Minnesota 56003.
www.capstonepub.com

122014
008658R

 Books published by Capstone Press are manufactured with paper
containing at least 10 percent post-consumer waste.

Library of Congress Cataloging-in-Publication Data
Biskup, Agnieszka.
    Hockey : how it works / by Agnieszka Biskup.
        p. cm. — (Sports Illustrated Kids. the science of sports)
    Includes bibliographical references and index.
    Summary: "Describes the science behind the sport of hockey, including skating, shooting,
goaltending, and the rink" — Provided by publisher.
        ISBN 978-1-4296-4023-7 (library binding)
        ISBN 978-1-4296-4874-5 (paperback)
    1. Hockey — Juvenile literature. 2. Sports sciences — Juvenile literature. I. Title. II. Series.
GV847.25.B47 2010
796.355 — dc22   2009042285

Editorial Credits
Anthony Wacholtz, editor; Ted Williams and Tracy Davies, designers;
    Jo Miller, media researcher; Eric Manske, production specialist

Many of the statistics in this book came from Alain Haché's *The Physics of Hockey*.

Design Elements
Shutterstock/Eray Haciosmanoglu; kamphi

Photo Credits
Capstone Press/Farhana Hossain, 7
Capstone Studio/Karon Dubke, 41 (top and middle)
Central Michigan University/Peggy Brisbane, 42
Getty Images Inc./Al Bello, 45 (bottom); Andy Devlin, 43; Bruce Bennett, 12 (bottom), 39 (bottom);
    Dave Sandford, 44 (bottom); Jeff Gross, 34; Jeff Vinnick, 29; John Giamundo, 17 (bottom)
iStockphoto/francisblack, cover (background)
NHLI via Getty Images Inc./Andy Devlin, 33; Mike Stobe, 23
Shutterstock/7505811966, cover (puck); Dainis Derics, cover (net); Dusty Cline, 17 (top); Sebastian
    Kaulitzki, 35; waya, cover (rink)
Sports Illustrated/Al Tielemans, 13; Bob Rosato, 26; Damian Strohmeyer, cover (left), 44 (top);
    David E. Klutho, cover (middle), 1, 3, 4, 6, 8, 9, 10, 11, 12 (top), 14, 15, 16 (top), 18, 20 (top),
    21, 22, 28, 30, 31, 32, 37, 38, 41 (bottom), 45 (top); Hy Peskin, 20 (bottom); Robert Beck,
    cover (top and right), 16 (bottom), 24, 25, 27, 36, 39 (top); Simon Bruty, 19, 40

TABLE OF CONTENTS

▷ INTO THE GAME

What makes hockey so exciting? Could it be the explosive slap shots that slam into the net as the crowd roars? Or is it the bone-jarring body checks between rival players on the ice? For a lot of people, it's all about the fast-paced action of the game. The players move so quickly that the game is constantly changing. Speed produces more scoring opportunities, more collisions, and a lot more action.

reaction time
The goalie must have quick reflexes to block the puck.

4

Science can help explain how all these exciting actions work. You can learn why a puck bounces, why mid-ice collisions generate so much force, and why the game moves so fast.

endurance
Skaters build up endurance through training so they can be strong on the ice for long periods of time.

friction
The blades on hockey skates help reduce friction, allowing the players to move on the ice.

CHAPTER 1

What makes hockey so fast? The ice! The slipperiness of frozen water helps pucks slide and players skate across the rink. Slipperiness cuts down on **FRICTION**. Friction slows down pucks and players. But what makes ice so slippery?

Scientists once believed that **PRESSURE** on the ice from a skater's weight melted the ice. This allowed the skater to slip and slide along a thin layer of water. While this is true, the change is much too small to be the main reason for ice's slipperiness.

Another idea was that a fast-moving skater creates heat with the blades on the ice. The friction could produce enough heat to melt a thin layer of water to slide on. But this idea didn't explain why a person standing still on ice could slip too. So what's the story behind the slippery nature of ice?

FRICTION — the force that opposes the motion of an object
PRESSURE — a force applied to a gas, liquid, or solid by another gas, liquid, or solid

Ice has a liquid film of vibrating water molecules on its surface. This film makes ice slippery, even at temperatures of minus 400 degrees Fahrenheit (minus 240 degrees Celsius). But at lower temperatures, this layer gets thinner, making it harder to skate when it's really cold outside.

IT'S THE LITTLE THINGS

Everything in the universe is made up of tiny particles called atoms. Atoms join to make groups called molecules. A water molecule, for example, is made up of one atom of oxygen and two atoms of hydrogen. Water can exist as solid ice, liquid water, or a gas. Molecules in a solid stick together in an organized pattern. They're locked in place and move very little. In liquids, the molecules are still close, but not as tightly packed together as in a solid. They can slip and slide over one another. In a gas, the molecules are very far apart and move around freely.

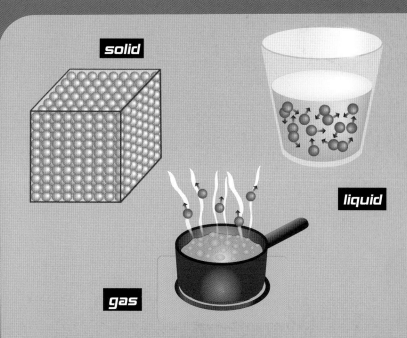

solid

liquid

gas

AROUND THE RINK

Making ice cubes in your freezer is easy. Creating an entire sheet of ice in an indoor arena is a little trickier. The technology for both is almost the same. The system is just a lot bigger for an ice rink.

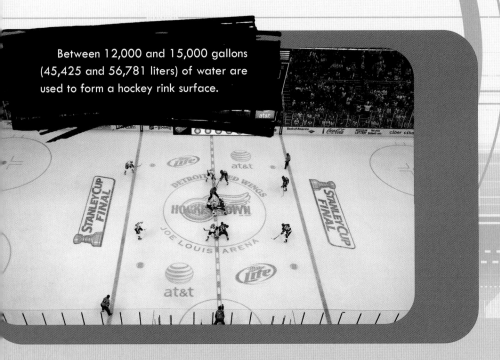

Between 12,000 and 15,000 gallons (45,425 and 56,781 liters) of water are used to form a hockey rink surface.

Most arenas use huge compressors to refrigerate and pump really cold brine, or salt water, under the rink. This action chills a concrete slab, upon which the ice is formed. They use brine because it freezes well below 32 degrees Fahrenheit (0 degrees Celsius), making the slab very cold. The brine is carried through pipes buried in the slab.

Once the slab is cold enough, the first few layers of water are spread, and the ice-making process begins. When the ice is .13 inch (.3 centimeter) thick, the crew paints it white. Otherwise the ice would look gray. More layers of ice are then built up. Then they paint on the lines, circles, and logos. More layers of ice are built on top of that until the ice is 1 inch (2.5 centimeters) thick — just right for playing hockey! The ice is kept around 16 degrees Fahrenheit (minus 9 degrees Celsius).

Hockey players are picky about their ice. "Ice is everything," said retired Philadelphia Flyers center Jeremy Roenick. "Ice is the difference between scoring and not scoring." Hockey players describe ice as being "fast" or "slow." They prefer fast ice, which is hard, cold, and smooth. Fast ice allows them to skate and pass the puck quickly and easily. Slow ice is warmer and softer than fast ice.

UNDER PRESSURE

Hockey players also prefer the ice in certain cities. The hard and dense ice they like is found in places with cold and dry climates such as Edmonton, Canada. The soft and slushy ice they dislike is found in places with warm and humid climates such as in Florida. Humidity is a big problem. Moist air doesn't cool easily. At the St. Pete Times Forum in Tampa Bay, Florida, four huge dehumidifiers run constantly.

But dehumidifiers are not enough when steamy air rushes in as fans enter and exit. The staff at the Forum increase the air pressure inside the arena. Then the air from inside will flow out instead of in when a door is opened. It doesn't work perfectly, but the Forum's ice has improved since the change was made.

ZEROING IN ON THE ZAMBONI

Over the course of a high-speed hockey game, the ice gets a real workout. Skate blades and hockey sticks leave grooves and gouges. Snow shavings and ice chips start building up. The resulting rougher surface of the ice makes skates wobble and pucks bounce. The rough ice slows down the game. So after a period of 20 minutes, out comes the Zamboni, the giant ice-resurfacing machine, to the rescue.

Moving at a top speed of 9 miles (14.5 kilometers) per hour, the Zamboni is used to smooth and clean the ice. The machine has a huge blade, which gives the ice a close shave. A large horizontal screw collects the shavings so they don't pile up on the ice. A vertical screw propels them up into the snow tank, which is later emptied outside.

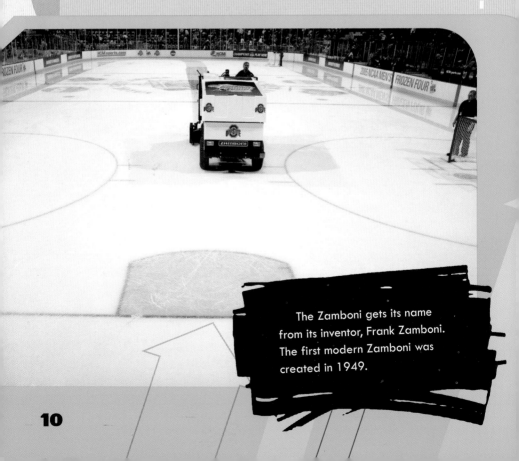

The Zamboni gets its name from its inventor, Frank Zamboni. The first modern Zamboni was created in 1949.

The machine has two water tanks. Water from the wash-water tank rinses the ice. The rinse loosens dirt and debris that accumulated on the surface. The dirty water is then collected, vacuumed, filtered, and returned to the tank. Clean, warm water from the ice-making tank is spread evenly across the ice by a giant towel. The warm water softens ruts and grooves. When the warm water refreezes, the surface becomes smooth again.

ZAMBONI MILEAGE

On average, a Zamboni covers .75 mile (1 kilometer) when resurfacing a hockey rink one time. With four resurfaces per game, the machine travels about 3 miles (4.8 kilometers) each game.

CHAPTER 2

▷ KNOWING THE GEAR

Ice skates were once made only of leather and plastic. Today they are made of high-tech **COMPOSITES** and **SYNTHETICS**. These skates are lighter, stronger, and stiffer than before. The boot material provides support. It also protects the foot from whizzing pucks and cuts from the blades of other players' skates.

The rounded shape at the front and back end of the stainless steel blade helps skaters make sharp turns. A flat blade, like the kind that speed skaters use, tends to keep a straight line. Try rolling a coin along a carpet in a circular path. Now try to move a playing card along the carpet the same way. The rounded shape makes turning much easier.

COMPOSITE — something made up of many parts from different sources

SYNTHETIC — something that is manufactured or artificial rather than found in nature

SPEED SKATING

If speed is so important to the game, why don't hockey players use speed-skating skates? Speed skates are designed for fast forward motion, and the blades are much longer than the boots. The speed skates, known as clap skates, allow the blades to detach from the heel. This feature helps the blade remain in contact with the ice longer. The design also allows the leg to provide a longer push. This happens without increasing the ice friction on the blade. The added foot flexibility creates more leg power, not only at the ankle, but also at the hip. But the gliding surface of the skate is larger than the hockey skate, meaning that the skater won't be able to turn as sharply.

Hockey players need to be able to move in all directions. They have to stop and start suddenly. For these reasons, hockey skates have less gliding surface. The players aren't able to skate as fast, but they can make sharp turns.

clap skates

If you look carefully at the bottom of a hockey skate blade, you'll notice that the surface is **CONCAVE**. The bottom of each blade has a groove with a sharp edge on each side. The edges give players the ability to dig into the ice. Then they can **ACCELERATE** quickly or stop on a dime. The wide, hollow groove helps prevent sideways motion while not sinking too deeply into the ice. Goalies prefer to have shallower grooves, since they need to move quickly from side to side.

CONCAVE — hollow and curved, like the inside of a bowl
ACCELERATE — to gain speed or speed up

STICKING AROUND

You can't play ice hockey without a stick. Players need them to shoot and pass the puck. Hockey sticks have a long, slender shaft. At the bottom, a flat surface called the blade is used to move the puck.

shaft

blade

A stick needs to be strong so it doesn't break during play. But more importantly, it needs to be flexible. The flexibility determines how much **ENERGY** the stick absorbs and transfers to the puck when shot. The energy is not directly transferred from the player to the puck. The stick bends and stores the energy before transferring it to the puck. This is similar to the energy held by a coiled spring. Shortly after hitting the puck, the shaft uncoils. The stored energy is transferred to the puck, causing it to travel at high speeds. In fact, hockey sticks are now designed to flex at certain areas along the shaft to increase puck speeds.

ENERGY — the ability to do work

Players don't always agree on what makes up the best stick. Some prefer longer, more flexible sticks. Some use sticks with blades that are curved at the tip. Others use sticks with blades that are curved in the middle.

Sticks were once all made of wood. Today sticks are also made of combinations of lighter and stronger materials. These include graphite, fiberglass, and Kevlar, which is used for bulletproof vests. Kevlar increases the **DURABILITY** of a stick without making it too heavy or less flexible.

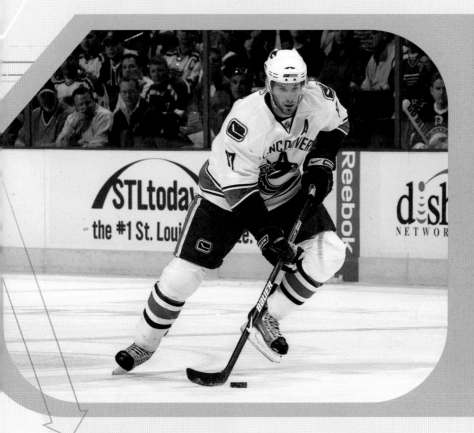

Blades are covered with friction tape to give a better grip on the puck. The tape has a rough surface, which holds the puck better than the smooth surface of the blade. Some players also put wax on the tape, which also makes the puck stick to the blade.

PICKING APART PUCKS

Because the game is so fast, the hockey puck rarely stops. Pucks are made of rubber, one of the bounciest materials on earth. Rubber is made up of coiled molecules that give it extra springiness. Pucks are made of vulcanized rubber, which makes them stiffer and less bouncy. Pucks are kept frozen before the game and between periods to make them even less bouncy. Frozen pucks also slide easier on the ice.

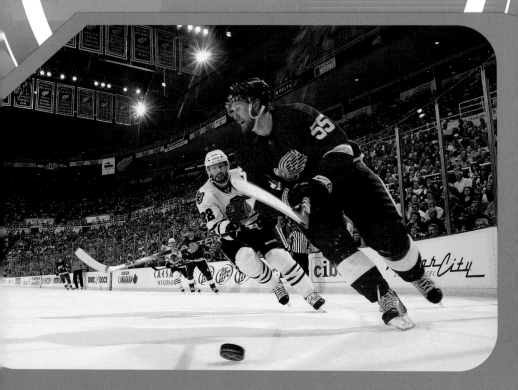

Puck Stats	
Color	Black
Material	Vulcanized (hardened) rubber
Weight	5.5 to 6 oz (156 to 170 g)
Size	3 in. (7.6 cm) in diameter; 1 in. (2.5 cm) thick

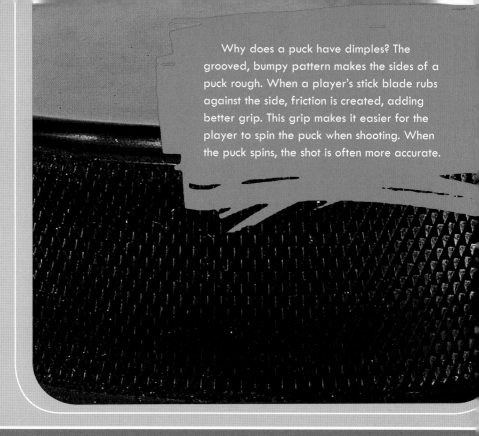

Why does a puck have dimples? The grooved, bumpy pattern makes the sides of a puck rough. When a player's stick blade rubs against the side, friction is created, adding better grip. This grip makes it easier for the player to spin the puck when shooting. When the puck spins, the shot is often more accurate.

NOW YOU SEE THEM, NOW YOU DON'T!

The puck moves around so fast during a hockey game that it can be hard to see. Fox TV tried to fix this problem during the 1995–1996 NHL season. It put computer chips in the pucks used in televised hockey games. Sensors tracked these FoxTrax pucks around the ice. The pucks appeared as glowing trails on TV screens.

Some players complained that the pucks handled differently than regular pucks. They argued that the FoxTrax pucks didn't keep cold as well and became bouncy more quickly. The FoxTrax pucks were soon history.

PLAYER GEAR

Hockey is a dangerous game. The ice is hard, the blades are razor sharp, and the puck whizzes at 100 miles (161 kilometers) per hour. The game is also full of physical contact. Hockey could never have developed into the fast, aggressive sport it is today without protective gear. The gear helps absorb the shocks during impact. It also helps distribute blows over a greater area.

Protective gear in hockey includes helmets, shoulder pads, elbow pads, shin pads, breezers, and gloves. Much of the gear is hard on the outside and soft on the inside. A hard, thin, outer plastic shell helps to redistribute the force of a hit. Inside the shell is a layer of soft foam that helps absorb the energy from a hit or fall.

SAFETY FIRST

Hockey players in the past wore few pads and no helmets. In 1979, the NHL made it a rule for all new players to wear protective helmets. The last helmetless player, Craig MacTavish, retired in 1997.

GOALIE GEAR

Of all the players on the ice, goalies need the most protection. Pucks traveling 100 miles (161 kilometers) per hour fly at them throughout the game. Their gear is specially designed to help them do their job while staying safe. However, the gear can weigh more than 50 pounds (23 kilograms).

WHO WAS THAT MASKED MAN?

Believe it or not, goalies were once expected to defend the net without a mask. Of course, this led to fractures, bruises, and many stitches. Montreal Canadiens goalie Jacques Plante changed all that.

During a game in 1959, Plante was hit hard in the face with a puck, breaking his nose. He refused to continue playing unless he could wear the fiberglass mask he wore during practice. After much arguing, Plante was allowed to play with the mask.

Not long after that, all goalies started wearing masks. Plante's style of mask is no longer used, but its fame continues. It became a popular horror symbol as the mask worn by Jason Voorhees in the *Friday the 13th* movies.

A goalie's chest protector has foam linings in the chest area. They cushion shots by breaking up the energy at the point of impact. They also help keep the puck from bouncing.

Goalie masks are made of light, strong materials. They can be made of carbon fiber or a fiberglass and Kevlar mix. They withstand the impacts of high-speed hockey pucks and spread out the impact of the puck. The chin and forehead pieces are designed to deflect pucks. The helmet's cage protects the goalie's face without affecting the goalie's view.

The goalie's pads are designed to deflect the puck. Even the graphics on the pads can be designed to create the illusion of a gap for a player to shoot into.

Goalie skates are different from standard hockey skates. The flatter, longer, and wider blades give the goalie more balance. They also make sideways motion easier. This freedom makes it easier for the goalie to protect the net. The longer blades make turning harder, but goalies don't often need to turn in tight circles.

A goalie's stick has a different angle between the heel of the blade and the shaft than a standard hockey stick does. It helps keep the blade on the ice. The wider blade also helps stop shots. Some goalie sticks are made of special mixtures of materials to absorb the puck's energy and reduce rebounds.

21

CHAPTER 3

▷ PLAYING THE GAME

You can't be a great hockey player without being able to skate. Hockey skating requires many quick changes of direction. Players have to be able to stop and start on a dime. These quick movements require explosive forces by a skater's lower body.

Hockey players skate with their knees bent to absorb the impact each time their blades touch the ice. Skating uses the foot, ankle, knee, and hip joints. Most of the energy the skater uses to move is released by the calves, quadriceps, hips, and buttocks. By swinging back and forth, the shoulders and torso help the legs deliver as much force and energy as possible.

For speed, players dig their skates into the ice and lean forward. This way, the legs exert a greater amount of force. But players can only lean forward during acceleration. If they tried to lean forward while traveling at a constant speed or slowing down, they would fall over.

Hockey players usually use three kinds of skating techniques during a game:

1) Free skating is the quick skating players use on open ice.
2) Agility skating uses explosive speed, fast direction changes, and quick stops and starts.
3) Backward skating is used to cover opponents without

MAKING THE PASS

Passing is the simplest way to move a puck in a straight line across the ice. Passing can move the puck down the rink much faster than the quickest skater can. For the most part, the puck stays in contact with the ice the whole time during a pass.

When a pass sets up a goal, it is called an assist. Up to two assists may be credited per goal. They are part of a player's stats.

If two players are standing still or moving in the same direction at the same speed, passing is pretty simple. But that's not very common during a game. A player might have to pass the puck to a teammate who is skating ahead. In cases like these, the passer can't aim for where the receiver is. Instead, the passer must aim for where the receiver will be.

So what's the best way to make a pass? First, the passer should put his main hand lower on the stick to give the pass more power. He should then shift his weight to his back leg and keep his head up to see where he wants to pass. With his target in sight, the player should transfer his weight from his back leg to his front leg as he makes a sweeping motion with the stick. During the follow-through, the player should try to point the stick at the target for a more accurate pass.

SLAP SHOT SCIENCE

Slap shots are a hockey player's fastest and most powerful shots. These shots can send the puck zooming faster than 100 miles (161 kilometers) per hour. To shoot one, a player raises the stick in a full backswing. He then slaps the puck with a long follow-through.

Shooters like slap shots because they are hard for goalies to see and stop. A goalie only has a few hundred milliseconds to make a save. The speed of the stick contributes to the speed of the puck, but it's the flexing of the stick that really harnesses the energy. The stick blade hits the ice just before it hits the puck. The player's weight bends the stick, loading the stick with more energy. At the peak of impact, a stick can bend by as much as 30 degrees. The bent stick shaft snaps back to its original shape — if it doesn't break! The stored energy is then released into the puck.

30°

SPEEDY PUCKS

At the 2009 All-Star game, Boston Bruins defenseman Zdeno Chara broke a 16-year NHL record. During a skills competition, he used a slap shot to hit the puck 105.4 miles (169.6 kilometers) per hour!

HE SHOOTS – HE SCORES!

Slap shots aren't the only shots hockey players use to score a goal. Players also use wrist and backhand shots to get the puck by the goalie. Wrist shots are made with a quick snap of the wrist, using little or no backswing. Wrist shots don't move as fast as slap shots. The energy in a wrist shot is released in a sweeping motion rather than a long wind-up motion.

Wrist shots, however, are more accurate. In a wrist shot, the puck is in contact with the blade longer. The puck can be guided more easily in the right direction. Even though a wrist shot doesn't move as fast as a slap shot, it can have an element of surprise. When a goalie sees a player raising his stick in a big wind-up, he has time to get ready for a shot. A quick wrist shot near the net, though, doesn't take long to set up. The goalie will have less time to prepare for a save. Washington Capitals left wing Alexander Ovechkin is known for his precise wrist shots that can take goalies by surprise.

Backhand shots are similar to wrist shots, but players use the back of the blade instead. They can surprise a goalie because they are shot when the player is turned away from the net. Backhand shots can be difficult when using a stick with a lot of curve. The puck can roll off the side of the blade because the back of the blade is **CONVEX**.

CONVEX — curved outward, like the outside of a ball

MAKING THE SAVE

The goalie's job is to stop the opposing team from scoring goals. Goalies have quick reaction times, which help them make lightning-quick saves. They need to be flexible and have **AGILITY** to be able to block and cover shots.

Gear helps goalies too. Like a giant human shield, a goalie can cover much of the net just by standing still. In fact, their equipment can block more than 60 percent of the net.

But goalies have another trick up their sleeves. They can also work the angles to reduce the amount of net a shooter sees. If the goalie stays deep in the net, the shooter can see more of the net and has more places he can shoot. But if the goalie moves out of the crease and closer to the puck, the shooter will see less net.

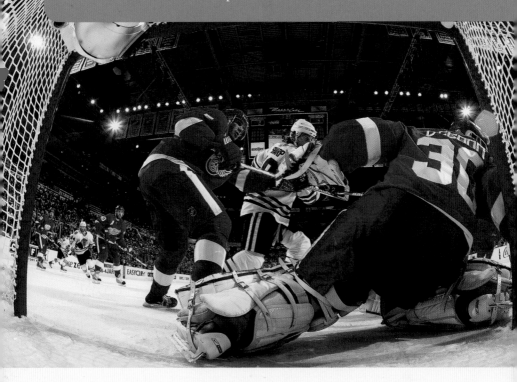

AGILITY — the ability to move quickly and easily

The goalie can also go down on the ice with his knees together and his legs spread out to cover the bottom of the net. This move is called the butterfly style because the goalie's pads look like a butterfly's wings. Vancouver Canucks star Roberto Luongo is considered to be a butterfly-style goalie. Some goalies use a combination of stand-up and butterfly styles to stop a puck. This is called the hybrid style. NHL goalie Martin Brodeur of the New Jersey Devils often uses the hybrid style.

Some players wrap black tape around the bottom of their sticks because it is the same color as the puck. They hope to hide the puck from the goalie's view.

THE EYES HAVE IT

Where should goalies be looking when they want to make a save? Should they look at the opposing player? Not according to a recent report from the University of Calgary. Researchers did a study of goalies to determine where they focused their eyes. They found that the best goaltenders kept their eyes on the same two things. These goalies focused on the puck and the shooter's stick for almost a full second before the shot. If they did that, they made the save more than 75 percent of the time. The eyes of rookie goalies, on the other hand, tended to wander. These goalies ended up having lower save percentages than ones who kept their eyes on the puck.

A COLLISION SPORT

Checking has always been a big part of hockey. This powerful act requires a lot of energy. The force in a check is a product of the mass of the players and the **VELOCITY** at which they're traveling at impact. The bigger the player is and the faster he's moving, the more energy is used.

It is the speed of hockey that makes it a dangerous sport. It is often considered more dangerous than football. In football, the players are usually larger, but they are moving at slower speeds than hockey players.

Players often check other players against the boards of the rink to gain possession of the puck. The boards are designed to absorb some of the energy of the impact. They bend a little when a player hits them. When they snap back into place, they send the energy back into the player, pushing him away from the boards.

VELOCITY — a measurement of both the speed and direction an object is moving

The most forceful collisions are delivered on the open ice. These impacts are less common than board checks. Open-ice hits tend to be more severe and cause more injuries. More energy is involved because both players are likely skating at greater velocities.

During a collision, **KINETIC ENERGY**, the energy of motion, is transferred. A player's kinetic energy is equal to one-half his mass times his velocity squared. A player with less mass than another player may still have more kinetic energy if he's moving fast enough.

Alex Burrows

Steve Staios

kinetic energy = ½ mass x velocity²

Steve Staios' kinetic energy: ½ (91 kg) x (3 m/sec)² = 410 joules
Alex Burrows' kinetic energy: ½ (86 kg) x (3.5 m/sec)² = 527 joules

KINETIC ENERGY — the energy of motion

GETTING HURT

Because hockey is a high-impact, fast-moving sport, injuries occur often. Players can get cuts, bruises, knee sprains, and dislocated shoulders. Many of the injuries are caused by fights, body checks, and collisions. When bodies collide, they don't just bounce off one another. The energy of the collision is transferred and absorbed by bones, tissues, and organs.

Concussions are one of the most serious injuries that players face. In a concussion, the force of impact causes the brain to slam against the skull. The impact sets off a chain of chemical reactions. These reactions can cause memory loss, headaches, balance problems, and even personality changes.

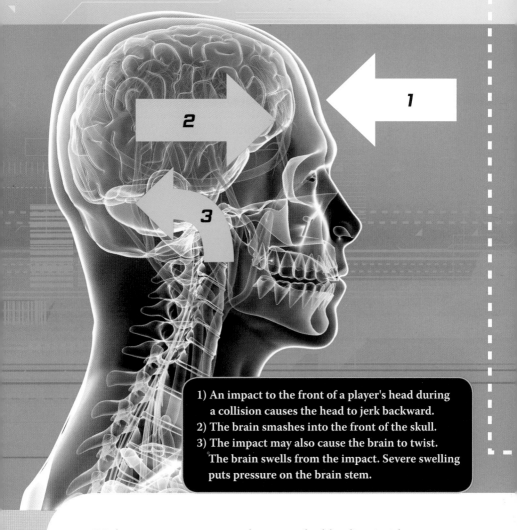

1) An impact to the front of a player's head during a collision causes the head to jerk backward.
2) The brain smashes into the front of the skull.
3) The impact may also cause the brain to twist. The brain swells from the impact. Severe swelling puts pressure on the brain stem.

With a severe concussion, there may be bleeding inside the head. A severe concussion can quickly become fatal. Repeated blows to the head can build up brain damage, which can also be fatal. Players wear helmets, but helmets can't always protect against the forces created by checking. Some experts recommend that fighting should be eliminated from hockey at all levels because it can lead to concussions.

CHAPTER 4

▷ BEING THE BEST

Hockey is an extremely intense game. Not only are players wearing many pounds of equipment, but they're also skating quickly. They forcefully swing their sticks to shoot goals. Every action they perform takes a lot of energy. Hockey superstar Bobby Hull once skated more than 8 miles (13 kilometers) in one 29-minute session during a game!

During the course of an average game, players can lose 5 to 8 pounds (2.3 to 3.6 kilograms). Most of the weight loss is water weight. Players have to constantly drink water to stay hydrated during the game. Over the course of a season, pro hockey players use so much energy that they can lose about 7 pounds (3.2 kilograms) of fat and lean body mass.

Because so much energy is used, NHL players take many short shifts on the ice rather than a few long ones. They can rest and regain energy between shifts so they can perform at a higher level. To stay fit, hockey players need both weight training and aerobics. Weight training strengthens the muscles, while aerobics helps build **ENDURANCE**.

ENDURANCE — the ability to keep doing an activity for long periods of time

Hockey players need to have well-balanced bodies. They use both upper and lower body strength in the game. Well-developed muscles help protect the body's joints and bones from injury. They also provide strength and power for skating, checking, and stick handling. Goalies spend extra time stretching their bodies to stay limber and to avoid possible injuries.

When you exercise, your body uses oxygen to replace energy. Running, bicycling, and swimming are examples of aerobic exercise. Aerobic exercise increases your heart rate. It is used during endurance activities.

Anaerobic exercise differs from aerobic exercise. During anaerobic exercise, your body demands more oxygen than your lungs and heart can supply. Then you start using the chemicals in your body for fuel. Your body can handle this kind of exercise for only short spurts of time because it is so intense. Sprinting, weight lifting, and resistance training are examples of anaerobic exercise. Hockey, with its quick stops and starts, is an anaerobic sport.

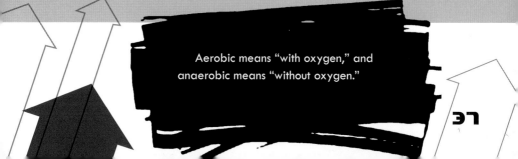

Aerobic means "with oxygen," and anaerobic means "without oxygen."

WHAT MAKES A PLAYER GREAT?

Wayne Gretzky is one of the greatest hockey players of all time. He was named the NHL's most valuable player nine times. He helped his teams win four Stanley Cups. By the time he retired in 1999, he set records in goals (894), assists (1,963), and points (2,857). Many people believe his records will never be broken.

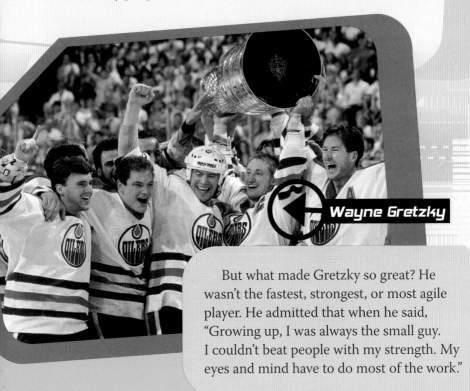

Wayne Gretzky

But what made Gretzky so great? He wasn't the fastest, strongest, or most agile player. He admitted that when he said, "Growing up, I was always the small guy. I couldn't beat people with my strength. My eyes and mind have to do most of the work."

What Gretzky did have was an ability to predict what was going to happen on the ice in the next few seconds of play. He said, "A good hockey player plays where the puck is. A great hockey player plays where the puck is going to be."

Gretzky was able to read the physical cues that other players dropped. He acted quickly to be in the right place and to make the right play. This ability is called field sense by coaches and perceptual ability by scientists.

People once thought perceptual ability was something great players were born with. But today, scientists believe this ability can be taught and improved through training. Human movement specialists are starting to find the clues that athletes need to make the right decisions. For example, by looking at the angle of a server's arm, tennis players should be able to tell where a ball will go.

Sidney Crosby

RISING STARS

Who will be the next Wayne Gretzky? A few years back, Gretzky was asked if he thought any player had a chance of beating his scoring records. He replied that Sidney Crosby was the best player he'd seen since Mario Lemieux. At the time, Crosby was only 15. In 2009, at age 21, Crosby became the youngest captain in NHL history to win the Stanley Cup.

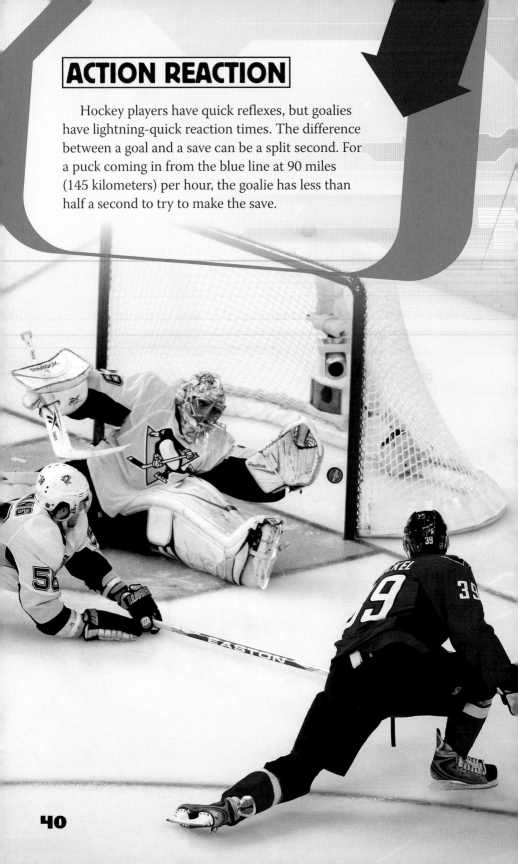

ACTION REACTION

Hockey players have quick reflexes, but goalies have lightning-quick reaction times. The difference between a goal and a save can be a split second. For a puck coming in from the blue line at 90 miles (145 kilometers) per hour, the goalie has less than half a second to try to make the save.

You can check your own reaction time by using a long ruler and some help from a friend. Have your friend hold the ruler with the bottom several feet above the floor. Place your thumb and index finger very near each side of the ruler's bottom, but don't touch the ruler. Have your friend release the ruler without warning, and try to catch it as quickly as possible. How quick was your reaction time?

Most people catch the ruler at around the 6- to 8-inch (15 to 20 centimeters) mark. Now compare that to a goalie's reaction time. To make a save for a puck moving 100 miles (161 kilometers) per hour from 20 feet (6.1 meters), the goalie has .137 seconds to react. With the ruler exercise, the goalie would have caught the ruler at 3.6 inches (9 centimeters). Now that's fast!

SCIENCE HELPING HOCKEY

Science has already helped improve hockey, but it can help even more. New research and studies may lead to better skates, better materials for gear, and even better players.

COOL UNIFORM

Even though hockey players are playing in an ice rink, they still get hot and sweaty. Manufacturers try to develop new fabrics that will be lighter and help keep players cooler. But how do they know they'll work? In Reebok's case, they take their new uniforms to Central Michigan University for testing. Scientists there study the heat patterns of hockey players wearing the new high-tech jerseys. They use a thermal camera and a body scanner to capture the images. The research is used to find out which uniform worked best to limit players' sweat and heat during a game.

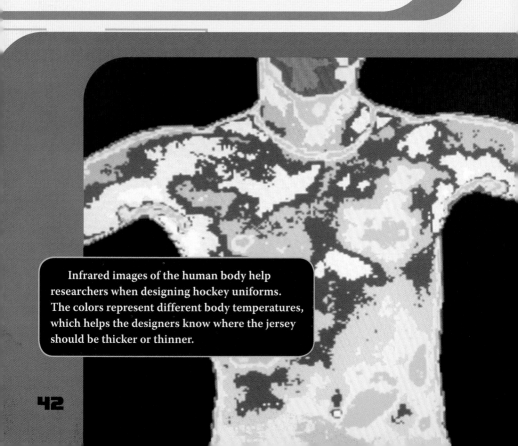

Infrared images of the human body help researchers when designing hockey uniforms. The colors represent different body temperatures, which helps the designers know where the jersey should be thicker or thinner.

HOT BLADE

The Thermablade, a heated skate blade with a rechargeable battery, is now on the market. The battery heats up the blade to 41 degrees Fahrenheit (5 degrees Celsius). The heat creates a layer of melted water for easier gliding. The ice becomes more slippery, reducing the friction between the blade and the ice. According to the manufacturer's claims, skaters will have quicker starts, tighter turns, and more speed out of turns. They won't have to work as hard to attain the same speeds, either. NHL players are currently testing the skates.

BRAIN TRAIN

Scientists from the University of Montreal are training the brains of hockey players and other athletes with special brain exercises. They are trying to improve the players' speed and accuracy in making decisions. In one exercise, for example, players tracked multiple objects as they moved around. The researchers have reported positive results. The athletes' ability to process information quickly and correctly increased on average by 53 percent after the training.

▷ FUN AND FAST HOCKEY FACTS

Hockey has been played for more than 100 years. The game is filled with a rich history, interesting statistics, and amazing facts.

Imagine a 240-pound (109-kilogram) player skating at half his top speed. He loses energy as he comes to a stop after checking a player against the boards. The energy lost can power a household light bulb for 60 seconds.

The best shooters can send a puck flying at speeds more than 100 miles (161 kilometers) per hour. If it's not stopped by the end of a rink, a puck shot at that speed on the ice would travel almost 2 miles (3.2 kilometers) in just over 2 minutes.

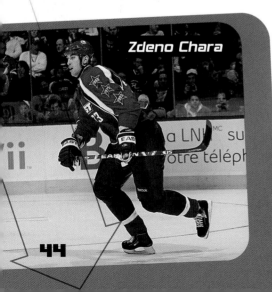

Zdeno Chara

When two average-sized players collide on the ice during a game, the collision can produce several thousand pounds of force.

At 6 feet, 9 inches (206 centimeters) tall without his skates, Zdeno Chara is the tallest player to ever play in the NHL.

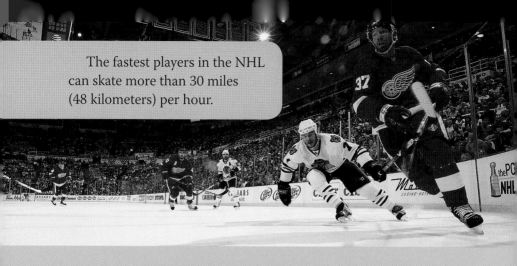

The fastest players in the NHL can skate more than 30 miles (48 kilometers) per hour.

Roy "Shrimp" Worters is credited as the NHL's shortest player at 5 feet, 3 inches (160 centimeters) tall. He played 12 seasons in the NHL as a goalie and was inducted into the Hockey Hall of Fame.

In the history of the NHL, only 11 goals have ever been scored by goalies. On February 15, 2000, Martin Brodeur became the only goalie to score a game-winning goal.

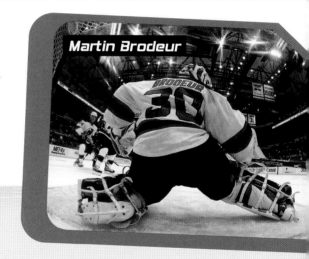

Martin Brodeur

From body checks to slap shots, science helps explain all the thrilling things we see on the ice. Should a goalie keep his eyes on the shooter or the puck? What kind of ice is best to skate on? Which shot is the most powerful and why? Science helps answer all these questions and more. Understanding the science behind hockey can help players become the best they can be. See if it can help your game too!

GLOSSARY

accelerate (ak-SEL-uh-rate) — to gain speed or speed up

agility (uh-GI-luh-tee) — the ability to move quickly and easily

composite (kuhm-PAH-zuht) — made up of many parts from different sources

concave (kahn-KAYV) — hollow and curved, like the inside of a bowl

convex (kahn-VEKS) — curved outward, like the outside of a ball

durability (dur-ah-BI-luh-tee) — the ability to last for a long period of time

endurance (en-DUR-enss) — the ability to keep doing an activity for long periods of time

energy (EN-ur-jee) — the ability to do work

friction (FRIK-shuhn) — a force that opposes the motion of an object; there is less friction between two smooth surfaces than two rough surfaces.

kinetic energy (ki-NET-ik EN-ur-jee) — the energy of motion

pressure (PRESH-ur) — a force per unit of area applied to a gas, liquid, or solid by another gas, liquid, or solid

synthetic (sin-THET-ik) — something that is manufactured or artificial rather than found in nature

velocity (vuh-LOS-uh-tee) — a measurement of both the speed and direction an object is moving

Johnson, Tami. *Girls' Ice Hockey: Dominating the Rink.* Girls Got Game. Mankato, Minn.: Capstone Press, 2008.

Levine, Shar, and Leslie Johnstone. *Sports Science.* New York: Sterling, 2006.

Solway, Andrew. *Sports Science.* Why Science Matters. Chicago: Heinemann Library, 2009.

Thomas, Keltie. *How Hockey Works.* How Sports Work. Ontario, Toronto, Canada: Maple Tree Press, 2006.

INTERNET SITES

FactHound offers a safe, fun way to find Internet sites related to this book. All of the sites on Facthound have been researched by our staff.

Here's all you do:

Visit *www.facthound.com*

FactHound will fetch the best sites for you!

INDEX